A Fire Truck's Day

by Lily Schell
Illustrated by
Mike Byrne

BLASTOFF!
MISSIONS

BELLWETHER MEDIA
MINNEAPOLIS, MN

Blastoff! Missions takes you on a learning adventure! Colorful illustrations and exciting narratives highlight cool facts about our world and beyond. Read the mission goals and follow the narrative to gain knowledge, build reading skills, and have fun!

BLASTOFF! MISSIONS

Traditional Nonfiction

BLASTOFF! READERS

BLASTOFF! Beginners

BLASTOFF! DISCOVERY

BLASTOFF! MISSIONS

Narrative Nonfiction

Blastoff! Universe

MISSION GOALS

> FIND YOUR SIGHT WORDS IN THE BOOK.

> LEARN ABOUT THE DIFFERENT JOBS A FIRE TRUCK HAS.

> THINK OF QUESTIONS TO ASK WHILE YOU READ.

This edition first published in 2023 by Bellwether Media, Inc.

No part of this publication may be reproduced in whole or in part without written permission of the publisher. For information regarding permission, write to Bellwether Media, Inc., Attention: Permissions Department, 6012 Blue Circle Drive, Minnetonka, MN 55343.

Library of Congress Cataloging-in-Publication Data

Names: Schell, Lily, author.
Title: A fire truck's day / by Lily Schell.
Description: Minneapolis, MN : Bellwether Media, Inc., 2023. | Series: Blastoff! Missions: Machines at Work | Includes bibliographical references and index. | Audience: Ages 5-8 | Audience: Grades 2-3 | Summary: "Vibrant illustrations accompany information about the daily tasks of a fire truck. The narrative nonfiction text is intended for students in kindergarten through third grade."-- Provided by publisher.
Identifiers: LCCN 2022013757 (print) | LCCN 2022013758 (ebook) | ISBN 9781644876633 (library binding) | ISBN 9781648348471 (paperback) | ISBN 9781648347092 (ebook)
Subjects: LCSH: Fire engines--Juvenile literature.
Classification: LCC TH9372 .S34 2023 (print) | LCC TH9372 (ebook) | DDC 628.9/259--dc23/eng/20220407
LC record available at https://lccn.loc.gov/2022013757
LC ebook record available at https://lccn.loc.gov/2022013758

Editor: Betsy Rathburn   Designer: Andrea Schneider

Printed in the United States of America, North Mankato, MN.

This is **Blastoff Jimmy**! He is here to help you on your mission and share fun facts along the way!

Table of Contents

An Early Start

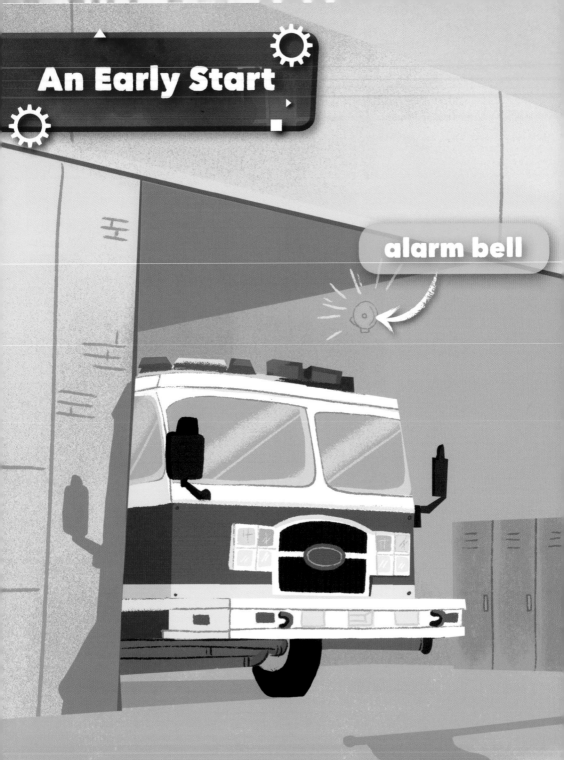

alarm bell

Ring! An alarm bell clangs in the fire station garage. A fire truck waits inside. The sun is not yet up. But the fire truck's day has already begun!

Firefighters rush toward the bright red truck. The driver climbs into the **cab** and starts the **engine**.

cab

▶ **JIMMY SAYS** ◀

Early fire trucks were painted red so they would stand out. Today, many fire trucks are bright red or bright yellow for the same reason.

firefighter

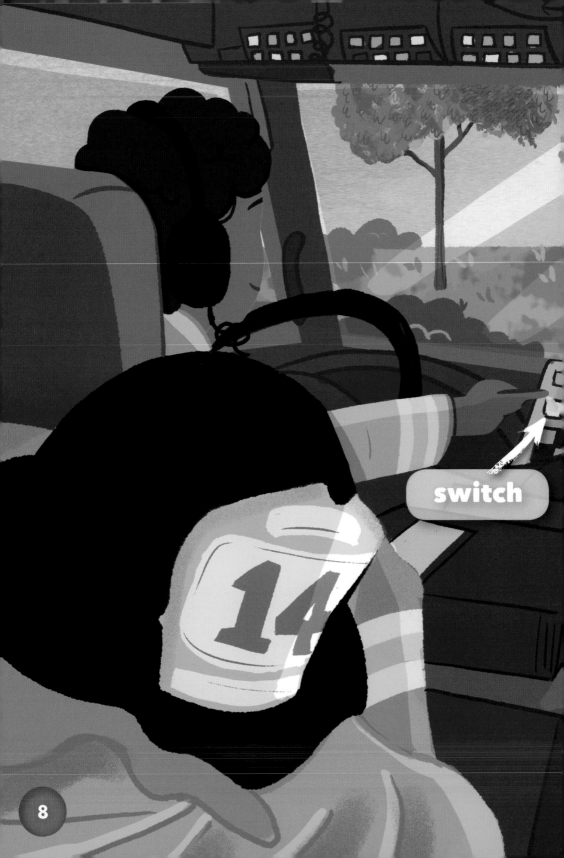

The driver flicks a switch and the truck's lights start to flash. He turns a dial and the **siren** wails. Out of the way!

10

traffic

The fire truck races to the scene of an **accident**. The driver parks the truck to block the road. The truck keeps **rescue** workers safe from **traffic**!

The firefighters run to help at the accident.

Soon, an **ambulance** and police cars arrive to take over. The firefighters climb into the truck and drive toward the fire station.

ambulance

police car

radio

A call comes in on the **radio**. There is a fire nearby!

The truck speeds to the building. Smoke pours out of one of the building's windows.

►JIMMY SAYS◄

There are several kinds of fire trucks. Some have very tall ladders on top to reach high places. Others are for wildfires!

helmet

mask

Two firefighters grab masks and helmets. They head into the building to rescue people.

fire hydrant

hose

Another firefighter grabs hoses from the truck. She connects one from the truck to a **fire hydrant**. She connects a **handline** to the truck. Now water will flow!

A firefighter takes a ladder from the truck. He leans it against the building and climbs up with the handline.

Another firefighter controls the **pump panel**. They put out the fire!

pump panel

handline

ladder

19

With the job done, the truck heads back to the fire station.

The firefighters spray and wash the truck. Now the truck is ready for another day!

20

Fire Truck Jobs

block traffic

carry masks and helmets

pump water

Glossary

accident–a sudden event that was unplanned and can cause damage or injury

ambulance–a vehicle used for moving sick or injured people

cab–the place where the driver sits

engine–the part of a fire truck that makes it go

fire hydrant–a pipe that goes to the street to provide water for putting out fires

handline–a hose used for putting out fires that connects to the fire truck

pump panel–the part of a fire truck that controls the flow of water

radio–a tool in fire trucks that helps firefighters send and receive messages

rescue–related to helping get people out of danger

siren–a tool that makes a loud noise in order to give a warning

traffic–cars, trucks, and other moving vehicles on a street

To Learn More

AT THE LIBRARY

Bowman, Chris. *Firefighters*. Minneapolis, Minn.: Bellwether Media, 2018.

Chriscoe, Sharon. *Fire Truck Dreams*. Philadelphia, Pa.: RP Kids, 2018.

Dickmann, Nancy. *Fire Trucks*. North Mankato, Minn.: Pebble, 2022.

ON THE WEB

FACTSURFER

Factsurfer.com gives you a safe, fun way to find more information.

1. Go to www.factsurfer.com.

2. Enter "fire trucks" into the search box and click 🔍.

3. Select your book cover to see a list of related content.

23

BEYOND THE MISSION

> WHAT WAS YOUR FAVORITE PART OF THE BOOK? WHY?

> WOULD YOU LIKE TO DRIVE A FIRE TRUCK? WHY OR WHY NOT?

> ADD A FEATURE TO A FIRE TRUCK. WHAT DOES IT DO? HOW DOES IT WORK?

Index